M O T D

MESSAGE OF THE DAY

Foreword

This book is a unique combination of self guidance and the exploration of spiritual practices through journaling and writing poetry.

First and foremost, this book is a journal for the user and an introduction to getting in-touch with your awareness and cultivating your wisdom through writing.

MOTD is an acronym for Message Of The Day and a regular practice that I have been doing for almost 8 years. I began writing messages of the day to cultivate my wisdom and share inspirational messages with my closest friends and family on my whatsapp groups. What I do is a form of journaling through poetry that allows me to get in touch with my awareness and write short messages of guidance from the soul.

This book includes powerful practices and blank pages to encourage the reader to 'check in' and write from their heart how they're feeling into poetry or short stories. Amongst the pages are also my poems and messages of the day that I have written over a period of time to demonstrate and encourage the reader to look within.

I believe these pages are filled with powerful enlightenment for the reader, not only to explore my poetry, but to be inspired to discover themselves through journaling, meditation and unfolding their story into the pages.

Content

Dedications

I always dedicate my books to my son and this book is no different;
he is the reason and drive for my ethics and why I strive to always do the work.

I would also like to dedicate this book to my brothers and sisters and my closest
friends. It was with them that MOTD's first began.

INSIDE YOU IS THE POWER OF PEACE

Release your authentic self
Cultivate your wisdom
One word at a time
One
Message
Of The
Day

———————◆•◀———————

Affirm

Consider your beliefs
What would you suggest is your north star?
Claim your inner most soul passions next to your north star (my own is my son, for him I claim my passions to their fullest extent). Your north star is the brightest star in your sky, the one thing that pushes you to achieve and aspire to be at your highest vibration.

Learning to harness yourself and be calm, can be key to centering the self and supporting your foundations of beliefs exponentially towards your passions. Trust in your truth and begin with who you are today. That is the work.
Breathe deep and hold for four seconds, then release slowly.

In this book there are pages titled "Check in" with prompts for you to write your thoughts and feelings/messages of the day. As you get through the book this will continue, but the prompts will disappear giving you full autonomy to unfold your authentic self and your story into the pages.

Now begin to flow just as you are...

I am_____

I am ready to release_____

I am deserving of _____

I am destined to become_____

———————◆•◀———————

RITUALS & ROUTINES

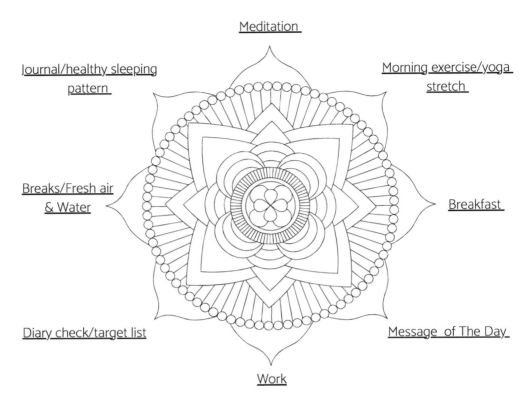

Meditation

Journal/healthy sleeping pattern

Morning exercise/yoga stretch

Breaks/Fresh air & Water

Breakfast

Diary check/target list

Message of The Day

Work

Beginning Meditation

Don't take the traditional poses of meditation, cross legged and prayer hands as the only way to meditate. It is only one of many possible positions to centre yourself and focus. Listening to your breath is the beginning, knowing and feeling the pace of your breathing and the rhythm of your heart, tuning in to your life force is where you start and where peace flows from.

The first move is to ignore what the mind believes meditation to be, in fact, do not concentrate on the mind at all, but tune into yourself. Lay flat on your back and allow yourself to listen to your breathing for 5, 10, or 15 minutes.

As you do this let the mind go and become the listener. Allow time to pass through you and focus on breathing from the diaphragm and exhaling fully. If it helps you can repeat a word like 'love' or 'peace' upon inhaling and exhaling to assist your focus.

Remember that you are not looking for silence. You are learning to listen to your life force, owning your focus and beginning the journey of the self. Any messages or reflections that come to the surface can be a sign of something to work on or to write about in your messages of the day journal.

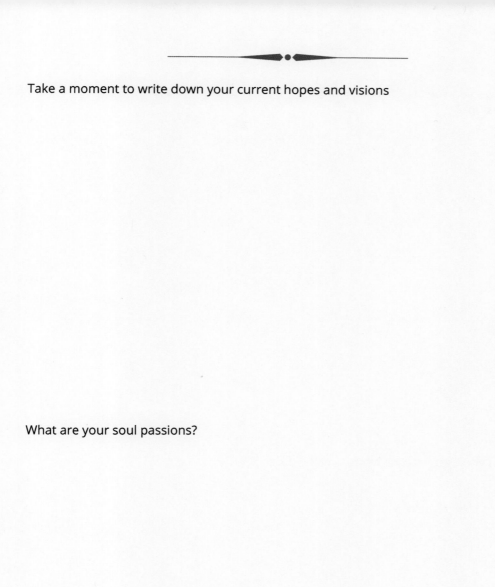

Take a moment to write down your current hopes and visions

What are your soul passions?

What goals can you set for yourself that will help you achieve your soul passions?

How can you best practice honesty with yourself?

GRATITUDE

Consider four or more things that you are grateful for. List each one, or create a short story or poem about them.

STRENGTH

Consider what you believe to be your strengths. List them out; it might help to create a short story or poem about strength.

MOTD

Elevate and
Alleviate
When we seek balance and,
Knowing of our inner self and,
Our soulfluid passions.
We release the strain that can regularly pretend to hold us up,
Scaffolding masks casting shadows attracting attention.
When we seek balance and,
Release
We elevate and alleviate
Capturing within space and,
The building blocks from our righteous and sincere beginnings,
Spirit levelled
Elevated
Toward aligned truths and,
Divine continuity

_ -J3- _

Check in

Continue to open up your awareness of self. Listen to your breathing for 5 minutes repeating the word 'Love' on the inhale and the exhale. Then when you are ready begin to write.

What are your weaknesses?

What are your fears?

How can you best practice self compassion?

Check In

Take a deep breath, breathe in and count down from 7 to 1, exhale fully and slowly then begin to unfold into the pages how your day has been.

MANTRA

Mantra

Sit for 10 or 15 minutes, listen to your breath perhaps play some calming music at a low volume.

Listen in your awareness and say quietly to yourself

"Unblock anything related to
Health
Love
Wealth and,
Success"

Repeat this as many times throughout your meditation whilst noticing your breathing.

The pace and intention that you say this with can really help the clearing of any blockages or negative thoughts and make way for a better manifestation process and positive vibration.
Say it slowly and from your heart noticing your life force and harnessing your strength in each of your words.

"Unblock anything related to
Health
Love
Wealth and,
Success"

Free-write - *to write without stopping or thinking (English dictionary definition). To write whatever comes up and make poetry of it (my definition).*

Try to free-write your own mantra below; it can be as many, or as few words as you like, or even a single word that you can say in your meditation while practing your breathing.

Some words of self compassion can help put feelings into focus and centre your mood. Take a deep breath and exhale slowly allowing yourself to really feel the release. Dig deep and start to write.

How do you feel about yourself?

Your light is your greatest asset
Freewrite...How do you best share your light?

Giving your heart and leading with love is the key
Freewrite...How do you best express what is in your heart?

How can you best practice sharing your authenticity and your truth? Freewrite below using the prompt words love and light.

Check in
Continue to flow, how did your day go?

MOTD

Real
Power
Lies
In the belief and,
Sensitivity
That
We
Are all
Infinite
Love
At the core
Of our
being

_-J3-_

SENSITIVITY ~ FREEWRITE

What are you sensitive to? Breathing through your triggers and the things we are sensitive to, listening to yourself without response allows you to take back your power and console your inner emotional wounds. Writing down what comes up can allow you to manage the mind and the heart to a place of calm.

MOTD

Embrace action and
Be the power within
Believe in yourself as the source and the prayer
In your awareness know you are greatness
Personified
There are few answers without first having lived so,
Say less
Embrace your light within the self
With compassion and grace
Share the vibrant light of unconditional that is you.

_-J3-_

ACTION ~ FREEWRITE

List ideas that you want to breathe action into, or write more about the progress of your aspirations and soul passions you wrote earlier in the book.

MOTD

Breathe life and,
Love into everything you do.
Lean in,
Allow time to push through the now
While you focus on your works and ambitions.
In you and of you
In front and becoming
Within
Grow,
With
Every
Breath
Breathe from your world within
Out to your endless becomings.

_-J3-_

What are your targets now? Freewrite below or create a poem about things you love to do.

YOUR WORLD WITHIN

See Yourself as the light at the centre, everything around you is possible
because you shine your light on it.
You are the abundant light.

Family
Peace   Love
Exercise   Faith
Compassion   Joy
Diet   Goals
Selfcare   Patience
Health   Light   Friendships
Respect   Goodness
Success   Support
Guidance   Kindness
Relationships   Opportunity
Resilience   Enthusiasm
Career

The light of your world within is your peace
Bloom into every location of your existence.

SYNCHRONICITY

MOTD

Cultivating inner synchronicity
to see the beauty in you
Manifest before you
Loving inward
Always unto you
The source
Or sauce
That ingredient like no other
A slow cooking is the progress and,
Every small small pinch of passion and,
Breath of reflection is touch, taste and beautiful.
The boundless power of self-love
Is a matter of releasing inward
Knowing you have power over nothing outside of you
Only synchronicity of self is the journey and beauty
Is the process to peace

_-J3-_

How do you synchronise and best align yourself with your truth?

Check in

FREEWRITE BELOW~ Take some time to remind yourself of your childhood, how would your younger self receive who you are today? Imagine you are having a conversation, what are some of the highlights you might share?

RELATIONSHIPS

MOTD

Love yourself into winning
The targets of your heart
Centre
Give your honesty and loyality
For your dreams and,
Your rewards, will be infinite.
Attracting balance;
Show up
In love and kindness, as you are
Allowing space and taking time
In gratitude and with free will
To receive and rise with abundance

_-J3-_

How do you love on yourself?

Self-care is the foundation of healthy relationships. Having a secure relationship with your self-awareness and cultivating your inner wisdom will allow you to see the best in others and offer the best of you. List some things you can do to show yourself more love.

Check in

How do you best share quality time and hold space with people you love?

With 'Self' at the centre, write all your family members and friends names on this page
Start with your family closest to you and work your way outward using the whole page!

Trust how you give to your 'Self' and then spread the love

Self-Motivated

Revitalised

Amplifying Energy

VIBRATION

Honesty

Will Power

Self-Elevation

BALANCE

Positive Well Being

PAGE OF INSPIRATION

Stability

Healthy Connections

Prosperity

Compassion

Strength

Warrior Spirit

Nobility

Good fortune

Unconditional Love

Heightened Intuition

Clarity

MOTD

Real art
Is the art of self
Unfolding your reflections and empowering from the spirit
Unpicking your trained charges of the previous
Knowing how to redraw and rewrite or free-write.
To release
Into new real art
To journal and mind map, draw and Recreate with
Recognition of the Levels of blessings we grow through
We are all, each of us
Real art and,
Each day
A new canvas to begin and,
Or continue
The masterpiece
That is the self

_-J3-_

Check in

MOTD

In the beauty of love emitted and,
Boundless in self
Only forward can be shaped into newness
For bliss is all around us should we lead
With openness, nature and nurture
If balance is synonymous with not having the answers, only the awareness,
Cherishing the relationships built
Within and without
Beliving in your truth is key
That the universe supports outwardly giving always in peace
Honesty sits upon lessons towards righteous hearts
Emitting light casting shadows off a kaleidoscopic world within
Releasing reflections of soul fluid passions in human form
Forward shaped into the awareness of how best to honour
The beauty of love emitted and,
Boundless in self

_ -J3- _

L
O
V
E

Check in

Writing messages of the day is sometimes like writing love notes to yourself, reminding yourself how you love who you've become or are becoming. Its about sharing love outwardly with yourself. Daily spiritual writing can unlock your love and free will and teach you to think with your heart when moving forward and treating yourself with care.

What do you love most about yourself?

I am...

Courageous
Tenacious
Generous
Kind
Friendly
Adventurous
Trustworthy

LOVE - How do you best express yourself in matters of the heart?

Do you show up with your acts of service clear with your intentions and affections and without expectation, but lovingly and encouraging?

When you give gifts, do you do so without expectation, with a listening ear and a caring heart?

If quality time is what you desire most then how do you call upon it? How do you make it so it suits all party's needs? How do you best share what quality time means to you with the one you want to share quality time with?

Words of affirmations - Never underestimate the power of a morning message or a morning poem of how you dreamt of someone special. Sharing a message of good luck or an empowering message of the day to tell a friend they're amazing and that you're thankful for them can change the outset of another persons day and your own.

Physical touch is a matter of communication, sensitivity and two people being in sync with how they feel in the moment. Talking about what is pleasing or displeasing to one another, remembering that we are all naturally nervous beings and all have different histories and experiences with touching, kissing and sex, means physical touch can be something that either just works straight away, or takes some time to get right; in many cases it's the latter. Talking to one another and being sensitive and intentional can be helpful, but most of all being safe and finding out what works for each other can bring harmony and allow for the best experiences.

MOTD

Succeed in love and legacy
What you have within,
Expand on it with vim
Build forward on purpose with vigour
For evolution in self is clear.
Live for love from the light within and,
Offer self in order of everything that counts and,
The response will be that love and humanity
Grow and glow exponentially.
Make time for time to pass through
For effort to create space and,
Be creative and spontaneous;
Know that when you know it's meant for you
You choose those that choose you
With openness,
Live in every ounce of your worth and truth
Love unconditional, no expectations
Let actions fill the hearts of others and smiles endless
Set powerful spiritual principles and rituals to be embraced together.
Practice beauty, wholesome giving and being
Connect from near or far, with energy meet energy and,
Yet be still and know where you begin,
In gratitude and grace
Over-standing everything

_-J3-_

MOTD

Uniqueness
Is your platform,
Be
Everywhere, unique;
From soul passions to purpose evolution,
Express your inextinguishable light

_-ʒ3-_

How are you?

What is unique about the way you love?

MOTD

Know that your reach can be exponential
Owning your inner self, intuition and awareness
Heightening your practice of the unconditional within
Is the blessing of being at one without and one with all
The position of
I am,
In consciousness of everything
Being
Loved and,
Loving,
Being one interstitial essence of spirit
Moved daily in word.
Divine in limits
Ascending in belief of the self
Is the reach
Indefinable in love

_-J3-_

Check in

Write about or, list your feelings about love.
It could be about friends or a special person.
How do you best show up for your needs and, how do you best give space to other people's love language and what they require?

EXCEPTIONAL

MOTD

Exceptional
Being of greatness
Centred
Deserving and rewarded
In beauty and splendor
Aligned with wealth of inner faith and Compassion
You are seen
Heard and,
Appreciated in guidance
Blessed and infinite, paving the way toward greater.
Trust in your truth
Trust in your process

_-J3-_

MOTD

Whatever allows you
The freedom to centre
In all your might, that
Brings simultaneous joy and peace
Into your setup and compliments your vibrations
Into bliss
With your hand on heart, breathe;
Divine guidance shall show you your truth
In dreams before your eyes

_-ꝰ-_

FREEWRITE- FREEDOM AND PEACE

List some words that make you feel free and at peace

MOTD

Allow that which makes your spirit vibrate and lift your energy
To its highest ascension and,
Into the beyond.
From the starting point and when you first wake,
Toward forward movement of your life plan, in each new day
Without sight, sometimes only heard,
Only felt in the shadows.
That shift
Into the awakening;
Awaiting the light within to show you the bliss of your reflection,
Spellbound of your talent, that first thing your passion resembles,
Is the reveal.
The path to your creativity,
to open doors to hearts
And bless the path you're on.

_-J3-_

MOTD ~ ORDER

Offering
Reflection
Determination
Educate
Repeat...

See yourself
Authentic,
At the receiving and achieving of your goals in your own uniqueness and,
Splendour.
Accept yourself in full beauty and joy and surrounded by your blessings,
Then become,
To meet yourself as the only self,
The great achiever of your time;
For you and in you
The immediate blessings that receive you,
Whole and in hearts centred in clarity of self:
Offering
Reflection
Determination
Educate
Repeat

_-33-_

EQUANIMITY

MOTD

Evenness;
Even in this,
From all ends of equal
Shadows unwrap divinity,
Redefining change,
Especially when flooded with gratitude and grace.
Meditated for the space
Allowing for nature to unwrap the natural
The universe beginning to show you a never-ending in faith
For you to bet on you
In a whisper within your deepest water,
Still,
To trust it will provide light that
Nothing could disturb
The evolution into purpose, into new answers,
Some days without answers to enthuse the growth.
Into anticipation and then new
Strength elasticised for the right dispositions;
Balance transformations
Physically and mentally seeking
equanimity of self

_-J3-_

SOVEREIGNTY

MOTD ~ FREEWRITE

It is clear to me
That we are meant to be
A sovereign reign of energy,
A bountiful push and pull
With the confidence that we and I are backed up by universal flow.
I am stature
Greatness in manifestations and divine soul factor
A state of being to be,
Spreading love the way hearts centred to connect
A metamorphosis of free will.
Who do, what you do?
Call it what you will;
Magic on the sight of your presence,
You are a gift.
Openness is key for those who see themselves within pure of life
With acceptance of the divine,
Spiritually sovereign in health and wealth,
That each of us are a spirit in human
Being.
Energies combined
With a unique field of change, ego-less and shadow duality resigned,
In uniqueness and oneness.
Spirit vibrations,
Here to embody life's plan
To give voice and create expression into life span;
To all that is you was born into experience and expression,
Focus of consciousness and our differences combined
Is the height of sovereignty.

_-J3-_

How do you best embody sovereignty and openness?

MOTD

Breathe.
Listen within for truth and honour for exploration of self,
Dream out of your heart into life,
The release can only be for the forward growth.
The uplift,
The authentic, taking its place in higher purpose,
For cultivating of wisdom and awareness.
Lived
Is a reflection and a forefront meditation,
Into the path of self,
Shared for the soul-fluid connections
For the passion flow.
Breathe,
There is only the exploration with creativity
That allows the beauty to be seen in infinite truth and honour.

_-J3-_

MOTD

One cannot possess all the answers if at all any,
However if you let time move through you and,
apply yourself with grace and gratitude,
Toward the authentic in you,
and work on your soul lines and true vibes,
Feed spirit into your passions:
The universe will deliver on unfolding your journey
In divine timing, see,
Your soul knows what it is here to do and,
Harnessing your duality into non-existence and,
Loving fully who you are,
In oneness from the shadows to the light,
Will see you
Giant in human.

_-J3-_

Check in

Earlier you listed targets and your vision and talked of soul passions you wished
to manifest into existence and breath action into.
How is your progress?

HUMILITY

MOTD

Live and love in all with light, outwardly giving
Without the presence of fear nor the presence of past or future but,
On living in the now,
Live and love in the moments forward
Into the new,
Into the rest and,
The beauty of slow;
Know the self, enough to share without hesitation,
For humility, is the root-growth agent beautiful in humans.
Breathe spontaneity into reaction and,
Action deep like ocean floors of vulnerability.
Shifting worlds and will
I
Am
Futures.
Out of stardust meets the eyes and dreams of constellations connecting dots
Where energy meets the ancestors' guides,
For the soul knows the path of ethereal,
Allowing space
To teach and,
Growth to meet a new.
To be pure in Love and light
Centred in gratitude
Genuine;
Slow moving through with silent giant steps,
Filled with wisdom and powerful shifts under sky's flow,
As a retrograde slows by
To shift in light
Of changes that write futures
Into bliss.

_-J3-_

Check in

Continue to flow, how do you feel?

MOTD

Your purpose and vulnerability lie surface deep and unbound in the ocean of self:
Now swim,
Believe
Tread and spread beauty in the waves of your evolutionary transformations;
Let time flow, rapid through "I"
In aura, in awe, in one with mother nature...
Let your heart vibrate a wisdom like water from your feet to your crown
Astral to your awareness in mind
Be
Motion
Inside
Light
Outside
Returning current correcting on whirlpools and breaks of past lives into lagoons
and falls;
Be the fluid that breathes colours of faith
Of springs
Into the new.

_-J3-_

Check in

ALIGNMENT

MOTD

The real glow up
Is to shine your light
To not be swayed out of the feels as to
Who you are, but
To hold space in the natural release and let joy flow through,
To inspire and support
To know your alignment is in the poetry and,
Your heart is in the forward;
Shadows on display
From foot to crown
Holding balance in every way
To shine is offering peace
Knowing that grace is divine timing wrapped in compassion,
Fruit of the souls unfolding.
Giving
Holding and,
Letting flow
With the sun in your sign lighting the ways
Glowing towards infinite possibilities
Journeying toward your highest self.
The real glow up is the inspiration that is free in your light

_-J3-_

Check in

MOTD

To be
Compassion unfolding
Consciousness uploading and
Inspiration on tap
Is a vibration and a gift
To over-stand and withhold
That not all will be ready to receive, but
Those who see you will see you clear
All day every day
Know you're not for everyone, in truth
Know it well as a blessing and,
Feel it in the freedom
That to be all of the above
Is synonymous with having the courage to be disliked but, to
nonetheless pour into the self enough to give freely in
gratitude with inspiration on tap and,
Compassion unfolding
Seeking equanimity in the ubiquitous of
Unconditional love and
Recognition of togetherness at the borders of imperfection
For those who see you, will see you clear
Aligned with them as you align with you.

_-J3-_

SPONTANEITY

MOTD

That energetic honesty
Spontaneity that hugs the atmosphere
Like
The duplicity of joy
Achieving harmony
That works,
That instantaneously enlightens into clarity
A universal unlocking
Where inspiration waters the grounds
message,
So our feet transmit the salt for our hearts
to light a burst of enigmatic humanity
With a spring in every flow and,
A reflection of serenity
In every glow.

_ -J3- _

Freewrite

How are you feeling?

MOTD

The bountiful extensions of inner wealth
Is all within for the sharing,
Progressive passions out flowing from the glory that is you,
Infinitely outgrowing
Imperfections and differences maketh one,
A present,
Moment's aligned, gift wrapped
Giving and allowing the universe to unfold;
Surrender
Into a blissful belonging
A soul-fluid freedom
A will extended in belief
Knowing in peace
You are complete
In every single breath.

_-J3-_

Check in

MOTD

Holding space for it in faith
Ready for thriving knowing success sounds like risk
Open with pace allowing time for the unknown
Protecting peace with respect for the heart
Giving in the name of wealth and inner values,
health and strength,
Knowing the release is the power of
transformation, of maturity and balance
That consciousness knows nobody but the self;
Your power lies there in grace within,
Pouring love and allowing time to pass through
Staying open
Giving
In your work and,
Raising your light,
To lift up those that choose you
Offering space where auras meet and,
Blessings recognise blessings for the joy and
The peace

_-33-_

Write about your joys

MOTD

From where the spirit seeks the mystical
Let it dance
Let the moments and dots of intriguing adventure
Tweak the ego direction
Silence the mind and lead with your heart
Breathe humble intentions and unfold with passion,
Fluently,
Holding your balance
Letting time pass through and around
Mirror the joys from within, outwardly unconditional with acceptance
From where the spirits seeks the mystical
Chase your dreams.

_-J3-_

Check in

Is there anything you feel the need to release? Leave it on the page and trust the process.

HONOUR

MOTD

In the strength we all contain
There is a key relationship required with self,
In honouring your dreams and
Recognising the changes,
Identifying the evolution of purpose through growth.
Following what you're naturally passionate for, your creativity,
You learn to walk with it into the storms.
Know that your will, is a strength unbeknown by the tests set before you.
Test's that are all earthly, while you are God's image and a free spirit
Open in this universe, flowing in your strength
Always capable of prevailing triumphant
recognising stability is a mechanism of your vibration
Well aware of the falls, showered by the hearts climbs,
The love shared and the strength built by joys,
Unconditional in the giving,
To be centred, in the "I am" of self and,
Holding your worth
Is to know you are always learning
Always walking the path you was meant to
With trust in your truth.

_-ჳ3-_

Check in

MOTD

Perhaps peace is synonymous with amplified spirit
Vibration of anticipation not knowing what comes next but,
Having a strong relationship with your awareness
And an ear to cultivate wisdom
Into focus and risk
To pursue your wildest dreams in the midst of any loss
In the midst of anything and all
Just in the midst of being.
To know that the win is closer, and the fall,
Is always the awakening beauty that sets you off into the wilderness of transformation
For every breath you are new
With love and light within and,
No permission required to be yourself full and free, of spirit,
Heart of hearts
Perhaps peace is synonymous with the collective noise of nature and,
Music between the moments that fit your heartbeat
Simultaneously to another before sleep and,
Rhythm sections;
The stars matching
The constellation you are
As the sky looks down on all
Perhaps peace is synonymous in the work and
The rest and,
The grace
Of the beginning in every sound and the triumph in every breath of life unto life.

_-ꝛ-_

Check in

MOTD

Embrace
The intricacy
The essence of the pull
Less the static more the grounding,
The gravitas of your creativity
For it is intrinsic
To the serendipity in your being,
One with your path
Time passing through you and,
You focused, going anywhere with action and direction
Personified.
Synonymous with meaning
A message of the day
When you know that it's meant for you
Following intuitions, unknowns and whispers,
With wonder
With openness and poetry
Spiritual writing and scribing
No worries just
Fingerprints on screen, press.
Gravity's pull on the edge of exhilaration and growth
Living and standing in every ounce of your worth and truth
Unconditional, without expectations, only hearts grace and
Smiles as endless as possible;
In the joys of giving
Embracing the spiritual for the balance and,
The clarity sewn into the cloth of resonance
Since long before passed from the ancestors via soul-fire passions and spirit vibes
Shared for those who see you and, you see them celebrating life and being
Kenetic, evolving and unfolding purpose
Meeting energy
With energy

_-J3-_

CONSISTENCY

MOTD

A beautiful happening in each of us
if you can believe it
See the vividest of dreams never leave you and have nothing to do with sleep but,
Everything to do with triumphs and,
Changing pavements,
The balance of a beautiful risk
Unfolding the first half into the next
For purpose and healing is never linear but symbolic with the souls journey.
It was meant to go this way, unpredictable
Beautifully juxtaposed
For experience sake,
That shapes your new,
Into a road without markings
Yet, stop signs and triangular junctions signalling anything, is of course possible,
While maintaining within is impeccable to the outcome
For the longest dreams never leave and have little to do with sleep
Rest is a new-found discipline and,
A spiritual requirement mixed with yoga
To tune into the beautiful happening;
Added energy stretched around you to withhold and become
Into purpose,
Into consistency and clarity you worked for but,
Wasn't aware you already held the capacity to own
Or even won before you gamed.
However you arranged the time stamp
Manifested this beautiful happening in all corners
Possibilities always upon you
When prayed for within
Spoken and rested with a dream;
The journey is yours
On the edge is where you will awake.

_-J3-_

Check in

MOTD

True vision far reaching beyond the vistas but,
Felt like a moving force
Mountain climbing to reach rewards reflecting real values
Being like flow
Like ink off fingerprint now screen saved
Doing more to include purpose over paid
Equilibrium when it comes to delivery
Giving back on all fronts,
Soaring forward
balance within self then risking upon the constellations
Over a new moon and saying it loud
For direction
Knowing that the universe
Will deliver in God's name
For you in image is God like
A super manifester if you believe it.
It's all in the breathing
That collectively we are one giving back to the atmosphere
Seeking to improve and lean in on truth at the edge of our highest vibration
In the present we reign,
forward thinking in visions to achieve
To aspire and to uplift within
To gain peace is to inspire through the creative
Each of us a gift
To be inspired is to trust in vision
Sky over everything
Moments and music instrumental in nature
Toward your route,
Seeking,
Gaining in movement and,
Or traction and,
Or a unique reflection chancing on self,
Your story
From your dream perspective over everything
To become inspiration and fuel others into believing
To risk the vision of your truth

Check in

MOTD

Your feelings of doubts are
A mere shadow of consequence
Written in the context of only past tense;
Once we believe that trust is stronger
This allows our anxieties to become a mechanism to push through
Into that future tense
Of divinity's hold
That self-recognition into the present.
Guided In belief
Unknown but beautiful in bloom
Chancing on balance
Self-centre nurture and flourish
Breathe, into forward movement and beyond
Leaving behind only what was and,
Expanding on the capacity of possibilities;
Into the wonderful of moments unknown
Seeking meaning for contentment and peace
In contribution to the giving through work,
Believing and trusting on the will of
What is meant for you
Will be

_-JB-_

Check in

MOTD

For meaning over everything
To cherish and welcome freeness in the spiritual
Bask in the equanimity and heaven in self
The Powerful God Image in self
The passions and the falls
The falls to passion into the work
The regrowth and realignment all at the same time
For everything, go through
As time passes through you
Spoken aloud to ensure in its purity and rewritten
Over and again into new days
Never left without maturing on to a new page
Surface through,
Or windows,
I touch
Into pleasures
Loved then worked over into rework
Into faith then freewrite
Nothing that is meant for your story is supposed to be unwritten
or suppressed
or left out
Nothing is without but within
Meaning and everything encountered is part of the plan
As you are
You must do
For there is no undo
Only a journey toward peace, compassion and self love
Into blessings shapeless in you
Learning always
Loving always, releasing and realising your energy
Spiritually sovereign over and again,
every day
New with each breath
Guided through in each breath
Held by divinity's direction in meaning
From love

_-ჳʒ-_

Check in

MOTD

Knowing there is always more
Is recognising the infinite reflections of your God in you and others,
The overflowing compassion
That can begin and become from the heart centre
If you first practice self-love fiercely and,
Project that love and release to others and toward the work that you do,
With the understanding that we are all an extension and an insight into one another
There, that is the more
If I said attraction and connection is your aura recognising a reflection of its infinite
God image in another, would you then see yourself clear?
That is where the capacity and abundance for more lies
That is where together
We are one.

_-33-_

Check in

MOTD

Inkwell
Conversations with the consciousness into peace
Loving all dimensions of self
Knowing the work is, who you've become
Unto righteousness we walk seeking,
Heart centred for the journey I journal
Possibilities prosperous ready and unfolding
Grace flows like water, for summers' outburst ready
Bring it
Ink
Well
For meaning in every dot of time passing time
For doing the love work within
Shaking shadows and unmasking duality
In the present we are presents unto the survival of the universe
through celestial beings and in return the energy serves
Unto destinies
In words regurgitated from consciousness into sub
Unto intuition out of abundance
Ink to action
Into flow
With peace.

_-J3-_

Check in

MOTD

To be,
To stand out
Open and be free
Spiritual and claiming of your will
To know that who you are and who you're becoming is purpose
On purpose
Consciously and sub
Shaping future's
In the present mold
Molding so strengthened by every breath and break
In the beauty of your skin signature
Self
Joyous
Stardust of the nights' energy and the days'
Gratitude into jubilation
To be who you are made of and see your journey personified
Unfolding and relatable in every becoming
To inscribe changes in the path of newness so far into the next
With bliss in the standing out and the awakening
Transforming in the peculiar awkwardness of human
Open
Loving
Natural
From the centre of your joys
Spellbound into mystery and meaning over everything
To be still , but not to settle, instead to stand in vibration of your highest self
Steady
Open and free
Claiming all dimensions of your endless will.

_-J3-_

What are your final thoughts?

Consider how you have felt about keeping a regular journalling practice, what benefits have you learned?

Recommended Reading List

- The Shadow Effect - Deepak Chopra, Marianne Williamson & Debbie Ford

- King, Warrior, Magician Lover - Robert Moore & Doug Gillette

- The Untethered Soul: The Journey Beyond Yourself: Michael Singer

- The Way of The Superior Man - David Deida

- The Prophet - Kahlil Gibran

- Loyalty to Your Soul - H. Ronald Hulnick Phd & Mary R Hulnick Phd

- The Power of Now - Eckhart Tolle

- The Chimp Paradox - Prof Steve Peters

- Astonishing the Gods - Ben Okri

- The Alchemist - Paulo Coelho

- A Way of Being Free - Ben Okri

- Living an Examined Life - James Hollis Phd

- Through The Dark Wood - James Hollis Phd

- The Courage to Be disliked - Fumitake Koga, Ichiro Kishim

- Truce: Healing Your Heart After Disapointment - Rob Hill Snr

- Inward - Yung Pueblo

- Vibrate Higher - Lelia Dela

- The Yoga Sutra's of Pantanjali - The Book of the Spiritual Man - By Pantanjali

The book list above is a series of books I have read during 2020 and the first 6 months of 2021 while daily writing the MOTD's that feature in this book and managing myself with a Journal and meditation. Some of these books I listened to on audio while jogging or on long drives and they definitely assisted me in my process of ongoing inner wealth and spiritual writing and focusing through my spiritual practices.

Printed in Great Britain
by Amazon

22617126R00057